Touch With Love

Edited by
Louis M. Savary

Association Press
New York, N.Y.

Touch With Love

291 Broadway, New York, N.Y. 10007

Standard Book Number: 8096-1818-4
Library of Congress Catalog Card Number: 78-152900
Printed in the United States of America

ACKNOWLEDGMENTS

Grateful acknowledgment is made to:
Ballantine Books, Inc. for selections by R. D. Laing from *The Politics of Experience*, 1967; Donald Barthelme for selection from "Robert Kennedy Saved from Drowning," 1968; Challenge Press, Inc. for selections by Robert H. Rimmer from *The Rebellion of Yale Marratt*, 1964; Clube De Poesia Do Brasil for poem by André Carneiro from *An Introduction to Modern Brazilian Poetry*, 1954; Collier Books for selections by Bernard Gunther from *Sense Relaxation Below Your Mind*, 1968, and for selection by Alan W. Watts from *The Book: On the Taboo Against Knowing Who You Are*, 1966; *Creative Playthings* for selection by Sasha Morgenthaler; Doubleday & Company, Inc. for selection by Ira Einhorn from "From Data Collection to Pattern Recognition: The Sociology of the Now," in *Psychedelics*, ed. Bernard Aaronson and Humphry Osmond, 1970; Ira Einhorn for selection from "Change, Media, Communication," 1970; *Good Housekeeping* for the selection by Billy Graham from "The Joy of Family Life," 1969; Grove Press, Inc. for selections by William C. Schutz from *Joy: Expanding Human Awareness*, 1967; Harper & Row, Publishers for selection by Ashley Montagu from *The Direction of Human Development*, 1955; Ione Hill for permission to reprint poems from *Strangers Eye-Kiss*, 1969 and from *Three-Eyed Pieces*, 1967; *Hit-Parader* for selection by Janis Joplin; Alfred A. Knopf, Inc. for selection by Kahlil Gibran from

The Prophet, 1923; Little, Brown and Company for selection by J. D. Salinger from *Catcher in the Rye*, 1951; The Macmillan Company for selection by Arthur Koestler from *The Invisible Writing*, 1954, and for selection by Theodore Isaac Rubin from *Lisa and David*, 1961; McGraw-Hill Book Company for permission to reprint selection by Jane Howard from *Please Touch*, Copyright © 1970 by Jane Howard, and for permission to reprint selections by James C. Clark, Betty Dederich, Stanley Keleman, Alexander Lowen, Virginia Satir, William C. Schutz, Mary Whitehouse as quoted in Jane Howard's *Please Touch*. McGraw-Hill Book Company, 1970; W. W. Norton & Company, Inc. for selections by Paul Watzlawick, *et al.* from *Pragmatics of Human Communication*, 1967; Pantheon Books, Inc. for selection by Alan W. Watts from *Nature, Man, and Woman*, 1958; Richard M. Prodey for permission to reprint "Poetry" and "To My Wife"; *Psychiatry* for selection by Martin Buber from "Distance and Relation," 1957; Random House, Inc. for selection by Alvin Toffler from *Future Shock*, 1970; Alice Sullivan for permission to use her poem, "Take a Walk"; Tavistock Publications, Ltd. for selection by R. D. Laing from *The Divided Self*, 1960, and for selection by R. D. Laing from *Families of Schizophrenics, Vol 1*, 1964.

Photo Credits: Karen Becker, 8, 29, 33, 37, 76–77, 93, 96, 103, 123, 138; Leslie Becker, 26, 30, 104, 132; Valentine Echo, 69; Maury Englander, 91; Joseph Ferrara, 127; Laurence Fink, 98, 149; Finnish National Travel Office, 86; P. J. J. Fortin, 35, 62–63; Fortune Monte, 10, 12, 38–39, 61, 72–73, 94–95, 110, 119, 120, 128, 140–141, 153, 156; Sylvia Plachy, 17, 19, 48, 52, 55, 58–59, 64–65, 75, 78, 83, 88, 107, 112, 114–115, 116, 131, 135, 143, 144, 150; Abe Rezny, 42–43, 56; Shelly Rusten, 20, 22–23, 25, 40–41, 44, 70, 100–101, 108; David Sagarin, 46–47, 66–67, 81, 84, 136–137, 154; Swedish National Travel Office, 14–15, 50–51; Swiss National Tourist Office, 124, 146, 159.

Contents

Preface

The word *touch* has many meanings. Touching involves muscles and sinews and skin. More importantly, it involves everything that goes to make up a sensitive person and a loving one.

If we are to reach the unawakened forces in one another, if we are to expand our awareness of ourselves and one another, if we are to experience a sense of solidarity with the human community, then we must learn to touch.

Touch has much to do with love, primarily because love implies contact, closeness, communion. Humans are flesh and bones and blood as well as spirit.

This book is about human sensitivity and understanding. It explores the many ways that we touch one another, and help shape the lives of those around us. The criticism is true that today we have lost much of the joy and enthusiasm of living. We have learned to discount life and forfeit hope. Part of the reason is that we have become socialized and conditioned to fear the touch of other people, or to make our touching something mechanical or subhuman, or even violent.

We must learn not only to touch, but to *touch with love.*

The first breath

We were born for joy, for spontaneity, for loving. Children are in a way symbols of a life free and without fear. Instinctively, their hands reach out to touch. They welcome the warmth of human contact. They like to feel, to be held, supported, cared for.

I suppose it all started when Ethan was born. . . . He emerged via natural childbirth, Lamaze method, and I was there. I saw him enter the world, get turned upside down, cry a little and then stop, get cleaned off, wrapped up, and put into my arms.

As I looked at him, he was very quiet and very curious. He lay quite still, concentrating on the "blooming, buzzing confusion," apparently entranced. For an hour we held him, and he was warm and close and peaceful. I even found myself trying to explain what he was getting into—and he listened carefully. I kept thinking that this might be the most important hour of his life. What a way to begin, by giving joy to parents!

The joy continues.

William C. Schutz

The baby is born with the need
for contact with other human beings.
He feels the need to be close to his mother,
an object of her love and the center of her activity.
He absorbs the tenderness of his surroundings,
learns in time to respond to it,
but is not yet capable of forming
an active relationship with another human being.

Sasha Morgenthaler

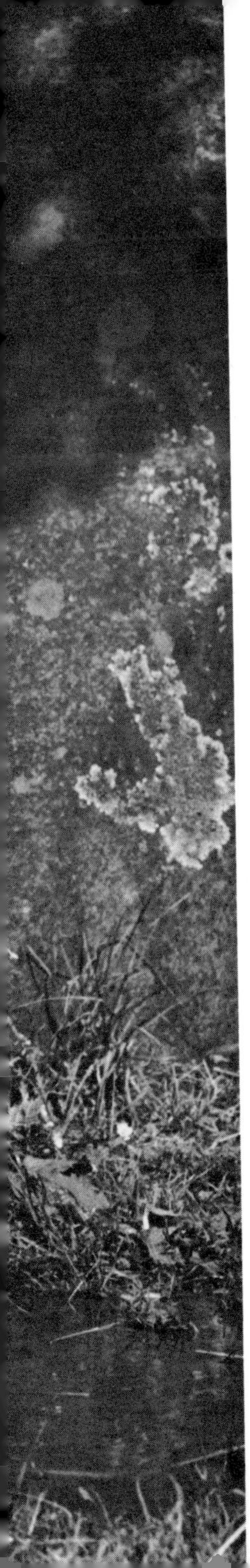

O blessed vision! happy child!
Thou art so exquisitely wild,
I think of thee with many fears
For what may be thy lot in future years.

William Wordsworth

Mother love is unconditional affirmation
of the child's life, his needs.
This affirmation of the child's life has two aspects;
one is the care and responsibility
absolutely necessary for the preservation
of the child's life and his growth.
The other aspect goes further
than mere preservation.
It is the attitude which instills in the child
a love for living,
which gives him the feeling:
it is good to be alive,
it is good to be a little boy or girl,
it is good to be on this earth!

Erich Fromm

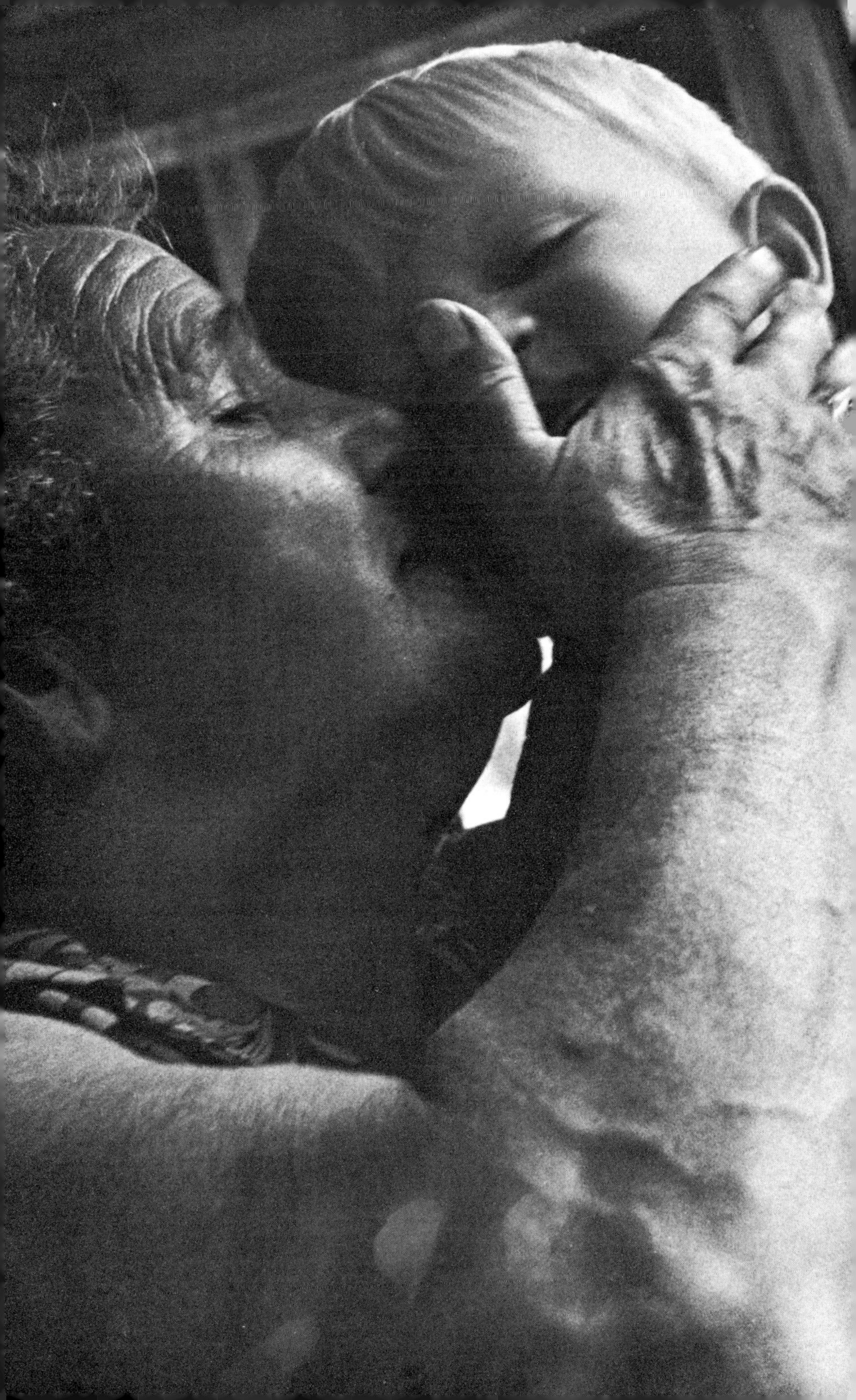

As adults, we have forgotten
most of our childhood,
not only its contents but its flavor;
as men of the world,
we hardly know of the existence
of the inner world:
we barely remember our dreams,
and make little sense of them
when we do;
as for our bodies,
we retain just sufficient proprioceptive sensations
to coordinate our movements
and to ensure the minimal requirements
for biosocial survival . . .
beyond that, little or nothing.
Our capacity to think,
except in the service
of what we are dangerously deluded
in supposing is our self-interest
and in conformity with common sense,
is pitifully limited:
our capacity even to see, hear,
touch, taste and smell
is so shrouded in veils of mystification
that an intensive discipline of unlearning
is necessary for *anyone*
before one can begin
to experience the world afresh,
with innocence, truth and love.

R. D. Laing

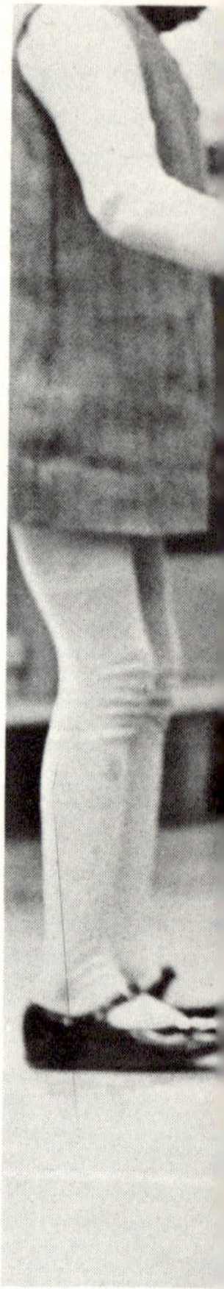

I was a sensitive child.
I had lots of hurts
and confusions.
You know, it's hard
when you're a kid
to be different.
You're all full of things,
and you don't know
what it's about.

Janis Joplin

NO PARKING

Alienated adults

At a certain point early in life we stop touching. We are taught to stop. People—children among them—learn to stay away from one another, to keep their hands to themselves. Spontaneity becomes inhibited, fears develop, resistance grows. People begin to drift away from one another, and break apart within themselves, their bodies alienated from their minds.

Originally the ego includes everything,
later it detaches from itself
the external world.
The ego-feeling we are aware of now
is thus only a shrunken vestige
of a far more extensive feeling—
a feeling which embraced the universe
and expressed an inseparable connection
of the ego with the external world.

Sigmund Freud

Lots of
people
with no
symptoms
at all
are
dying.

Anonymous

Men do not become
what by nature they are meant to be,
but what society makes them. . . .
Generous feelings . . . are, as it were,
shrunk up, seared, violently wrenched,
and amputated to fit us
for our intercourse with the world,
something in the manner
that beggars maim and mutilate their children
to make them fit
for their future situation in life.

Thomas Holcroft

Life is a fight against Nothingness.

Gabriel Marcel

Man is the dwarf of himself.
Once he was permeated
and dissolved by spirit.
He filled nature
with his overflowing currents.
Out from him sprang the sun and moon. . . .
The laws of his mind,
the periods of his actions
externalized themselves
into day and night,
into the year and the seasons.
But, having made for himself
this huge shell,
his waters retired;
he no longer fills the veins and veinlets;
he is shrunk to a drop.
He sees that the structure still fits him,
but fits him colossally.
Say, rather, once it fitted him,
now it corresponds to him
from far and on high.

Ralph Waldo Emerson

The feeling of being lonely
and very temporary visitors
in the universe
is in flat contradiction
to everything known about man. . . .
We do not "come into" this world;
we come *out* of it,
as leaves from a tree. . . .
Every individual is an expression
of the whole realm of nature,
a unique action of the total universe.
This fact is rarely, if ever,
experienced by most individuals.
Even those who know it to be true in theory
do not sense or feel it,
but continue to be aware of themselves
as isolated "egos" inside bags of skin.

Alan Watts

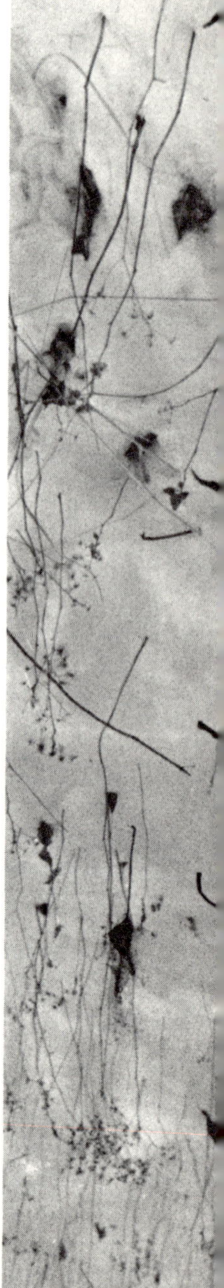

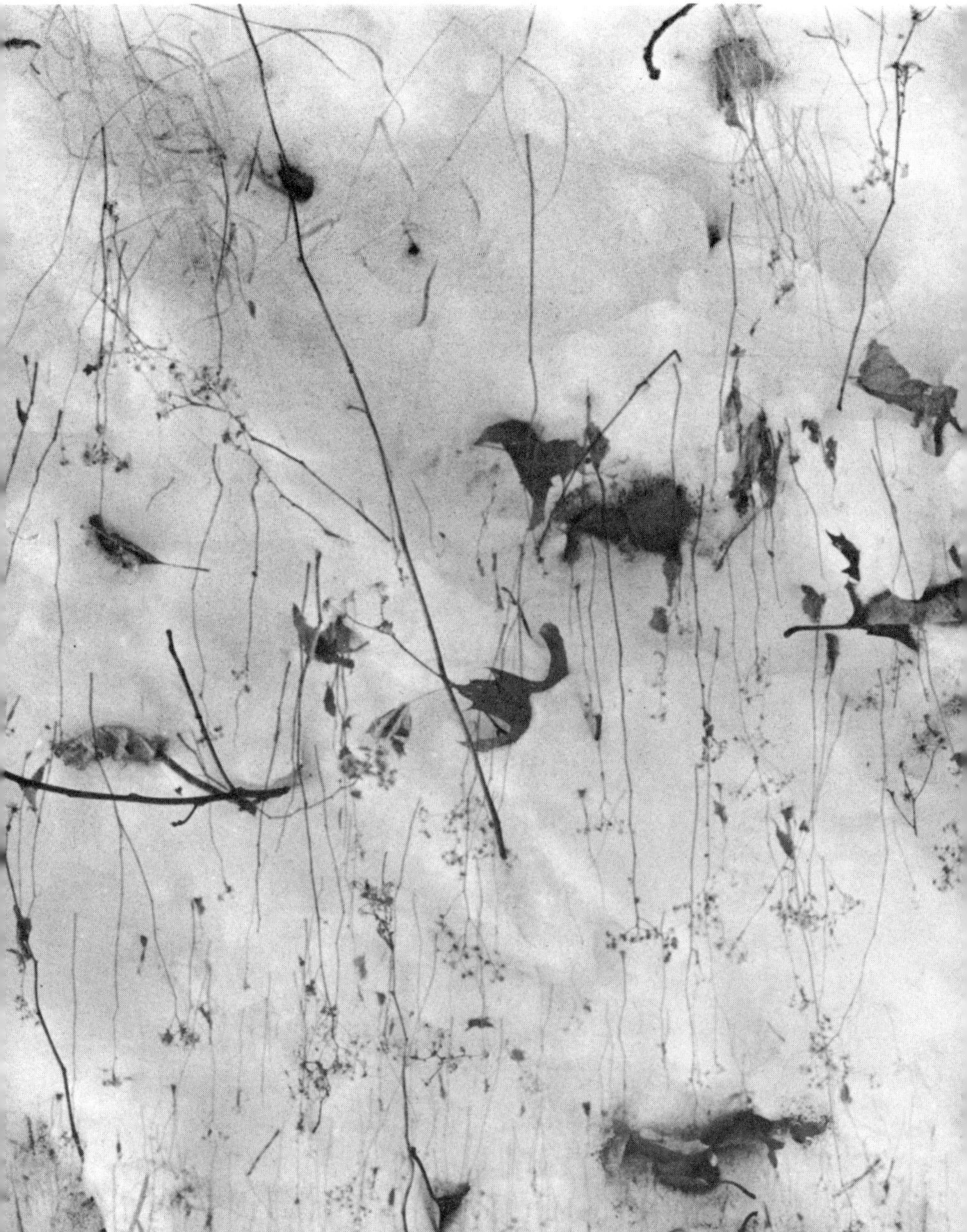

Without others

People are not meant to be alone, separated, alienated. Life is not meant to be without others. The universe and everything within it is created to be a loving unity, with everyone a part of it. Touch can help us toward this unity.

You can't think
when you're lonely.
Not coherently.
You just feel.
You feel the night,
moon-pale,
and the sky black.
You feel the smell
of Miami Bay.
The lonesome, dead smell
that the tide leaves behind.
It reminds you of other bays
and other tides,
and all you know
is that you wonder
what loneliness consists of,
and you know
that it is an aching
of the mind
that throbs through your body
as though part of you
had been torn away.

Robert H. Rimmer

No matter how one may try,
one cannot *not* communicate.
Activity or inactivity,
words or silence—
all have message value:
they influence others,
and these others, in turn,
cannot *not* respond
to these communications
and are thus themselves communicating. . . .
The man at a crowded lunch counter
who looks straight ahead
or the airplane passenger
who sits with his eyes closed
are both communicating
that they do not want
to speak to anybody or be spoken to,
and their neighbors usually "get the message"
and respond appropriately
by leaving them alone.

Paul Watzlawick

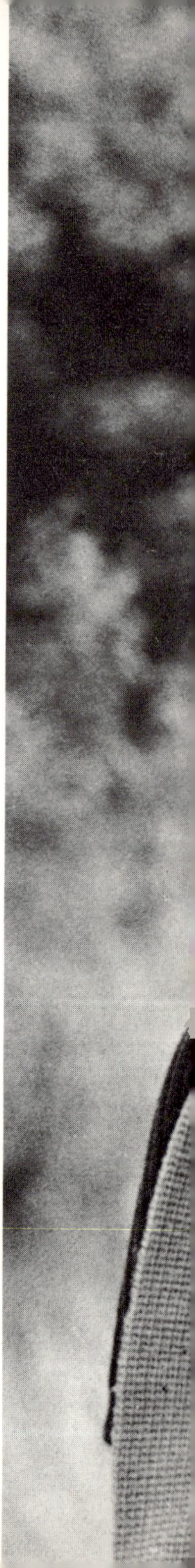

To be cut off
from other human beings
and their love,
to be cut off
from all sense of God
and of his love,
to be cut off
from what one believes
to be one's real self
and to be lodged
in the body of a ghost
who has lost the power to love:
this is loneliness.

Hubert Van Zeller

No more fiendish punishment
could be devised,
even were such a thing physically possible,
than that one should be
turned loose in society
and remain absolutely unnoticed
by all the members thereof.

William James

There weren't too many people in the zoo because it was sort of a lousy day, but there were a few around the sea lions' swimming pool and all. I started to go by it, but old Phoebe stopped and made out she was watching the sea lions. . . . I went up and sort of stood behind her and sort of put my hands on her shoulders, but she bent her knees and slid out from me—she can certainly be very snotty when she wants to. She kept standing there while the sea lions were being fed and I stood right behind her. I didn't put my hands on her shoulders or anything because if I had she *really* would have beat it on me . . .

She wouldn't walk right next to me when we left the sea lions, but she didn't walk too far away. She sort of walked on one side of the sidewalk and I walked on the other side. It wasn't too gorgeous, but it was better than having her walk about a mile away from me, like before.

J. D. Salinger

Alive in joy

Realizing that we are alienated to the roots is not enough, we must become human beings again. This involves learning anew all the basic languages of touch and feeling, learning to communicate and even breathe with a new mentality, learning how to live in joy.

Most people *think* they feel
rather than *feel*.

Bernard Gunther

Poetry

A poem
is
do
re
me
celebrating
breathing
soft
to
re
alive.

Richard M. Prodey

It is not how much we have,
but how much we enjoy,
that makes happiness.

Charles H. Spurgeon

All of the animals
except man
know that the principal
business of life
is to enjoy it.

Samuel Butler

We know everything except
how to make democracy work
and what to do with ourselves.
We know everything except
what is most important for us to know.

Robert Hutchins

We are primitives
of an unknown culture.

Gary Snyder

Living bodies

Perhaps as we become one again with flesh and feelings, we can rediscover some of the bodily joy that was once possible to us as spontaneous children, and can begin to understand what it means to be alive.

> O let me teach you how to knit again
> This scattered corn into one mutual sheaf,
> These broken limbs again into one body.
>
> William Shakespeare

We live equally
out of our bodies
and out of our minds.

R. D. Laing

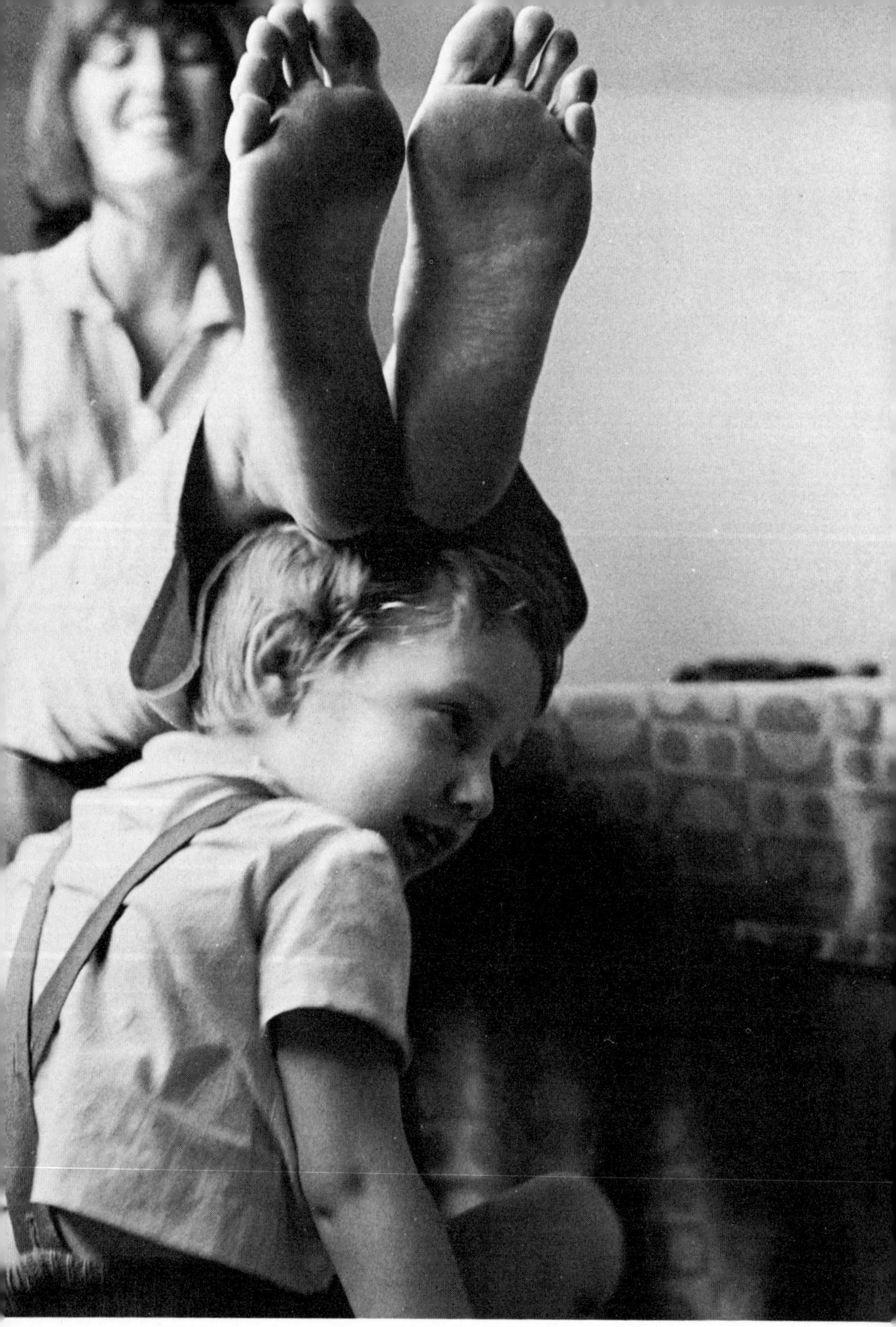

The human body
is not a thing
or substance,
given,
but a continuous creation.

Friedrich Nietzsche

We usually think of physical contact
as expressing only two things:
romance and utility.
We seldom touch each other
just for the sake of touching.
One of the terrible things in family life,
as soon as babies grow up,
is that people quit using what can be
one of the most helpful kinds of contact there is—
just using hands.
Adults can use hands
in so many other ways
than slapping, dragging,
pinching, pushing, pulling
or patting to mean "there-there."

Virginia Satir

The more you commit yourself
to any activity,
the more pleasure it will give you.
To commit yourself to life
is to commit yourself to your body.
We should let the body take over,
and not be so egotistically arrogant.
The body will heal itself.
It's a creation of nature.
If nature can't sustain life,
then nothing can.

Alexander Lowen

Touching things

The world is full of so many things that can really communicate to us only if we touch them: the rough bark of a tree, sand warmed by the sun, grass in early morning dew, or a smooth stone. Everything awaits the touch of human hands.

It is only a small planet
But how beautiful it is.

Robinson Jeffers

Take a walk
through the park
on a leaf-crunching
autumn day.

Inhale crisp air
chase a squirrel
  over a monument
skip around pigeons
crunch a leaf
take a drink
  of fountain water.

Watch for the morning sun,
or an evening sunset
  so rare
  in Manhattan.

Alice Sullivan

Even if I knew the world
were going to end tomorrow,
I would go out
and plant apple trees today.

Attributed to St. Francis of Assisi

Autumn clouds, vague and obscure;
The evening, lonely and chill.
I felt the dampness on my garments,
But saw no spot, and heard no sound of rain.

Po Chu-i

Light as the dart of a dragonfly
I touch your day face;
Soft as mothwing dust
I touch your night face,
Lest my frail shell
Crumble into abrasive;

As the pond lily catches
The morning sun in night-fallen dew,
I shall hold your day face
And your night face, find them one
In my cupped hands;

If I look at your face
In my cupped hands,
Will I see my own?

Ione Hill

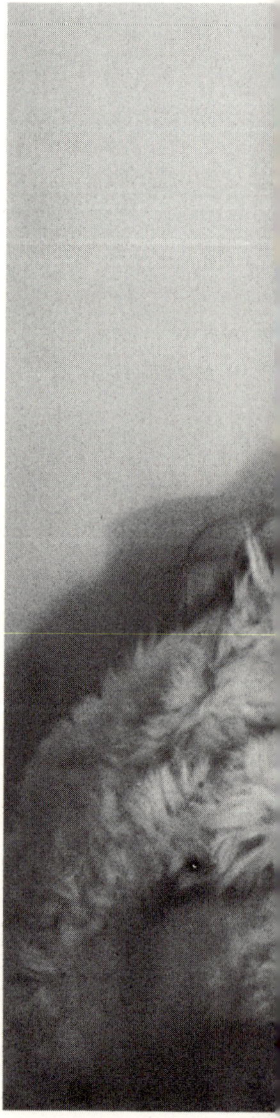

Water, quintessence of change,
mother of clouds and clay,
I feel your discreet presence,
transparent, inevitable.

Frozen prisoner
of the ice-box,
broad road of fishes,
damp tomb of the remains
rejected of man.

Made of anguish,
you spring from the eyes
by the rough road
of wrinkles.

You raise your red flag
on the breast of the wounded.

Water,
feelingly I drink
your voluptuous tastelessness,
your fine transparency.

André Carneiro

Touch and healing

We can discover, or rediscover, the power of touch. Many who have lost the ability to touch, to communicate their personal feelings to others, have suppressed in themselves a certain power to heal. To touch is to reach, and sometimes to help. And to be touched is to be reached, and sometimes to be helped, really helped, by another person.

He built a strong firewall
Of seasoned reason
Between
His mind and body.
Hear the wind
Rattle the shutters
Of the empty house.

Ione Hill

"What's the matter with you!
Can't you *feel*?"

Hasegawa

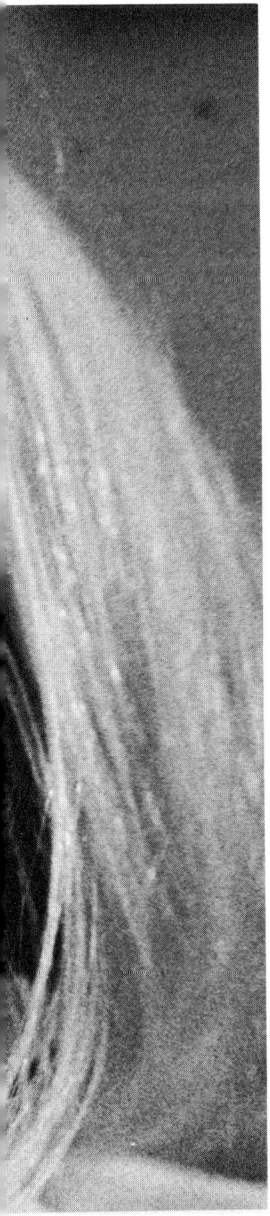

Awareness of feelings and emotions
allows experience to be felt
and integrated into the self.
The person who is open to experience,
and able to feel and appreciate,
has more experiential elements
than the constricted, denying individual
who cannot allow himself to feel deeply.

William C. Schutz

Touching and being touched
is a pleasure our culture
teaches us to keep away from.

Bernard Gunther

Children do not easily surrender
their habit of imagination,
their curiosity, dreaminess—
their awareness of mystery.
It is adults who eventually
force children to do that.

Samuel Willoughby

Spontaneity is, after all, total sincerity—
the whole being involved in the act
without the slightest reservation—
and as a rule the civilized adult
is goaded into it
only by abject despair,
intolerable suffering,
or imminent death.

Alan Watts

"Lisa, stay."
He spoke very slowly
and carefully.
Now he hesitated—then said,
"Lisa, trust me."
She looked up into his eyes. . . .
"Lisa."
He swallowed hard.
"Lisa, take my hand."

Theodore Isaac Rubin

Touch has always been
a most effective method
of healing.

Bernard Gunther

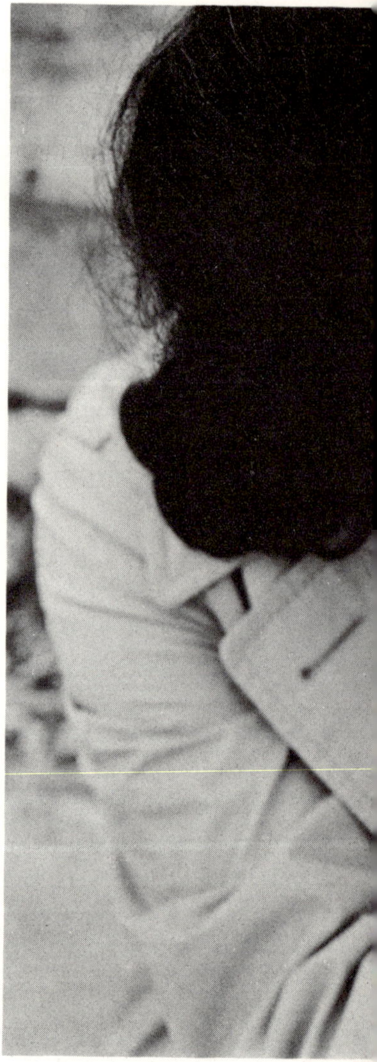

Inward, outward and beyond

In our inmost selves we do our living. It is false to say that what we are is simply the narrow surface of our conscious and voluntary selves. It is wholeness of being that creates the uniquely personal thrust of each self beyond itself to others.

This return to the sense of touch
is a regressive return
of energy
to a more integrative and immediate
mode of experiencing the world—
a mode that emerges from loosing the bonds
of the more distal senses (sight and sound)
producing a feeling of wholeness.

Ira Einhorn

We have in our time released
a totally new social force—
a stream of change so accelerated
that it influences our sense of time,
revolutionizes the tempo of daily life,
and affects the very way
we "feel" the world around us.
We no longer "feel" life
as men did in the past.
And this is the ultimate difference,
the distinction that separates
the truly contemporary man from all others.
For this acceleration lies behind
the impermanence—the transience—
that penetrates and tinctures our consciousness,
radically affecting the way
we relate to other people, to things,
to the entire universe of ideas, art and values.

Alvin Toffler

Movement can help change tension,
as much as relaxing can.
Movement is a river
you go swimming in,
it's the flow of energy
that carries you along.
What you find
as you work with the movement
is a dramatic physical
corroboration
of the pattern you know
is essentially true of you.
You get aware
of what's inward.

Mary Whitehouse

Each person
has his own touch,
like his own voice
or personality.

Bernard Gunther

There may be more beautiful times:
but this one is ours.

Jean-Paul Sartre

Earth's crammed with heaven
And every common bush afire with God;
And only he who sees takes off his shoes—
The rest sit round it and pluck blackberries.

Elizabeth Barrett Browning

Am I a harp
that the hand
of the mighty
may touch me,
or a flute
that his breath
may pass through me?

Kahlil Gibran

Thou mastering me
God! giver of breath and bread;
World's strand, sway of the sea;
Lord of living and dead;
Thou hast bound bones and veins in me,
fastened me flesh,
And after it almost unmade, what with dread,
Thy doing: and dost thou touch me afresh?
Over again I feel thy finger and find thee.

Gerard Manley Hopkins

Touched by others

In deeply personal communications between people, touch can mean much more than mere contact. It can mean transformation. Among lovers, the kiss is at once symbol and realization of a bond of love.

How does one soften
The tight prissy mouth?
Kissing may soften . . .
Who tightened the mouth?
Who knows?
Kissing may soften . . .

Ione Hill

First time he kissed me, he but only kissed
The fingers of this hand wherewith I write;
And ever since, it grew more clean and white,
Slow to world-greetings, quick with its "Oh, list,"
When the angels speak. A ring of amethyst
I could not wear here, plainer to my sight,
Than that first kiss. The second passed in height
The first, and sought the forehead, and half missed,
Half falling on the hair. O beyond meed!
That was the chrism of love, which love's own crown,
With sanctifying sweetness, did precede.
The third upon my lips was folded down
In perfect, purple state; since when, indeed,
I have been proud and said, "My love, my own."

Elizabeth Barrett Browning

If psychology pushed to its deepest truths
it could not stop short
of arriving at spiritual questions.
We need a new mythology
and a new set of symbols
to express modern man's
inchoate yearning for meanings
which can unite his experiences
on all levels.

Rollo May

ot Dog

The meeting of two personalities
is like the contact of two chemical substances:
if there is any reaction,
both are transformed.

Carl Jung

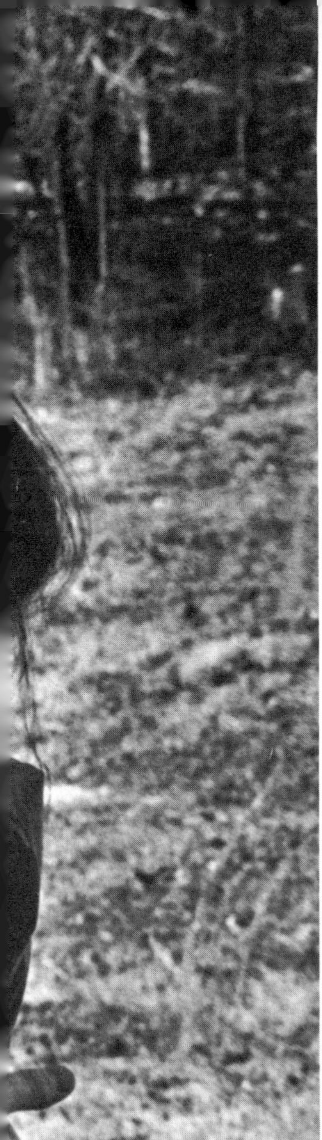

People sometimes say
"You can't change me in two days,"
and they're right; we can't.
But we can hope to change
what goes on between two people.
It's the interperson—our "usness"—
that is open to change and growth.
We can create the kind of climate
that allows people to tell each other,
as they never have before,
what's really going on with them.
Marriage partners
are always electrified
when they find that they have
twenty years of thoughts
hidden from each other.

James V. Clark

The rain is due to fall,
The wind blows softly.

The branches of the cinnamon are moving,
The begonias stir on the green mounds.

Bright are the flying leaves,
The falling flowers are many.

The wind lifted the dry dust,
And he is lifting the wet dust;
Here and there the wind moves everything.

He passes under light gauze
And touches me.

I am alone with the beating of my heart.

Lui Chi

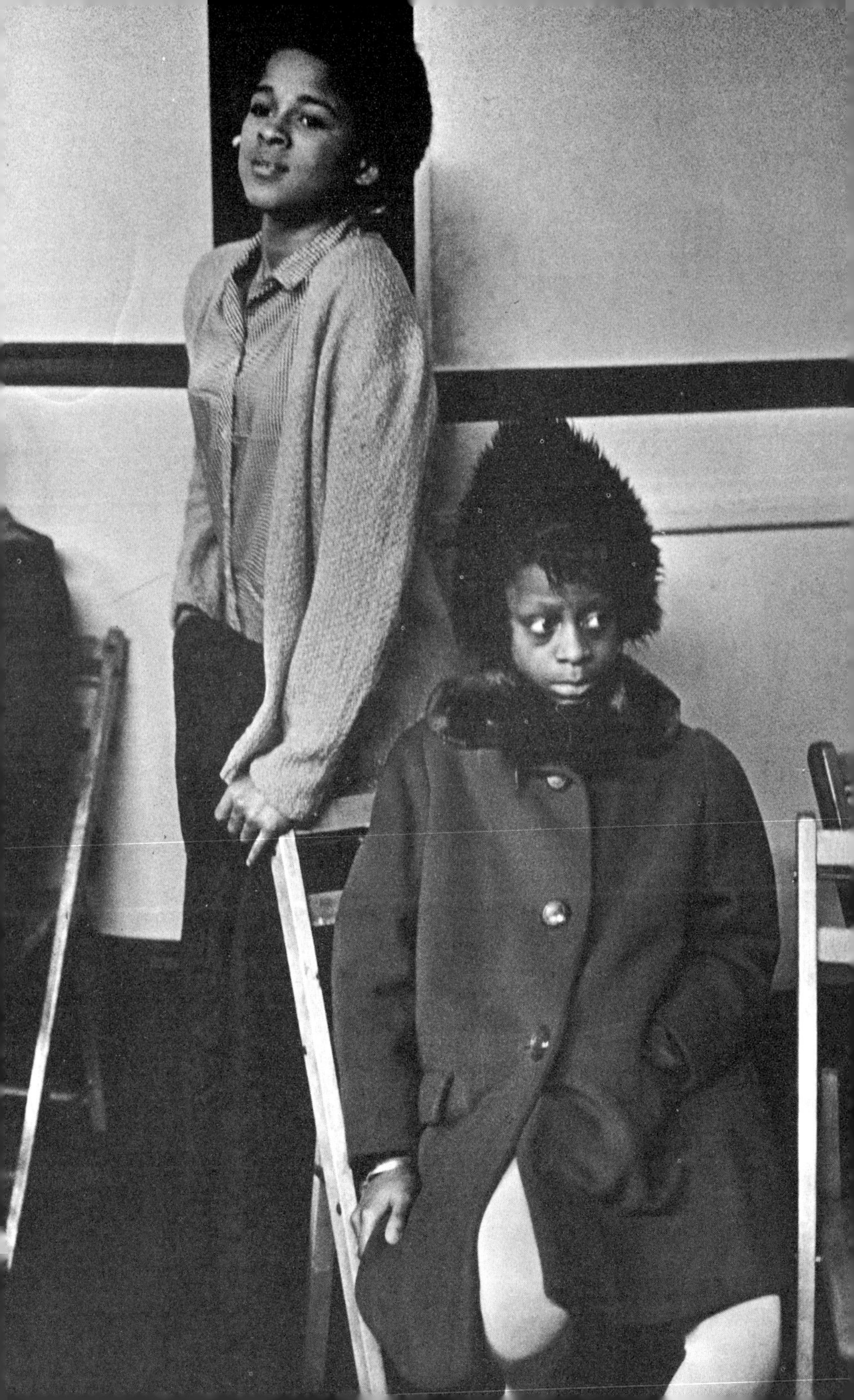

Silent communications

Human beings often communicate without words. We spend our lives sending silent messages, and some of these messages are important. True, often our nonverbal messages are never received. We send our signals out and listen for a response. Could it be that we ourselves too often insist on waiting for words?

If I should suddenly well up
And over, let me cry.

I have century's tears deep-frozen;
Your voice warm-touching my name
Could salt the frozen cloud to burst;
I've felt the melting
When your voice calling,
Gathers me to something meaningful
In this world of senseless transiency.

If you should say my name
And I should cry,
Do not question why,
Let me cry;

It won't be you who makes me cry
But you who lets me.

Ione Hill

Excessive verbal communication
is really the characteristic disease
of the West.
We are simply unable to stop it,
for when we are not talking to others,
we are compulsively thinking—
that is, talking subvocally to ourselves.

Alan Watts

2 MAGAZINES
POCKET BOOKS
Baseball
TEEN
For Men only
stag
MOVIE LIFE
modern screen
PHOTOPLAY
HOT ROD
SONG HITS
Air Progress
MOTOR TREND
MODERN ROMANCES
THE POPULATION BOMB
SAVANNAH EVENING PRESS
Seven Unsure Votes
Decision Wednesday

There are four wrong ways
people communicate.
You can blame,
you can placate,
you can be irrelevant
or you can be "reasonable."
There's something incomplete
about each way.
The blamer leaves out
what he feels
about the other person,
the placater leaves out
what he feels
about himself,
the reasonable one
leaves out what he *feels*
about the subject
being discussed,
and the irrelevant one
leaves out everything.

Virginia Satir

We have a great vocabulary
for hostility,
but we need new ways
to say "I love you."
Receiving affection
throws people into more of a crisis
than being yelled at.
People need both.
It's the sound of two hands clapping.

Betty Dederich

The puberty of the heart
precedes that of the body:
I had more need of loving
than of enjoying,
more desire for love
than for pleasure.
Today I cannot even imagine
the love of first adolescence,
when the senses are nothing
and the infinite alone holds sway.
Coming between childhood and youth,
it is the transition between them
and passes so quickly
that it is forgotten.

Gustave Flaubert

The basis of man's life with man is twofold,
and it is one—the wish of every man
to be confirmed as what he is,
even as what he can become, by men;
and the innate capacity of man
to confirm his fellow men in this way.
That this capacity lies
so immeasurably fallow
constitutes the real weakness
and questionableness
of the human race:
actual humanity exists
only where this capacity unfolds.

Martin Buber

The familiar system

The best-known communication feedback system is the family. And yet, time after time, people in the same family discover that they do not really know one another. These family memories and misunderstandings, crises and celebrations, are crucial in shaping the meanings of our lives.

> Interpersonal systems—
> stranger groups, marital couples,
> families . . .
> may be viewed as feedback loops,
> since the behavior of each person
> affects and is affected by
> the behavior of each other person.
>
> Paul Watzlawick

Vandergelder: "I had a talk with that artist of yours. He's a fool." Ermengarde starts to cry. "Weeping! Weeping! You can go down and weep for a while in New York where it won't be noticed. Ermengarde! I told him that when you were old enough to marry you'd marry someone who could support you. I've done you a good turn. You'll come and thank me when you're fifty."

Ermengarde: "But Uncle, I love him!"

Vandergelder: "I tell you you don't."

Ermengarde: "But I *do*!"

Vandergelder: "And I tell you you don't. Leave those things to me."

Ermengarde: "If I don't marry Ambrose I know I'll die."

Vandergelder: "What of?"

Ermengarde: "A broken heart."

Vandergelder: "Never heard of it. . . ."

Thornton Wilder

Family relations pertain to a plane
where the ordinary rules
of judgment and conduct
do not apply.

They are a labyrinth of tensions,
quarrels and reconciliations,
whose logic is self-contradictory,
whose ethics stem from a cozy jungle,
and whose values and criteria
are distorted like the curved space
of a self-contained universe.

It is a universe saturated with memories—
but memories from which
no lessons are drawn;
saturated with a past
which provides no guidance to the future.

For in this universe,
after each crisis and reconciliation,
time always starts afresh
and history is always
in the year zero.

Arthur Koestler

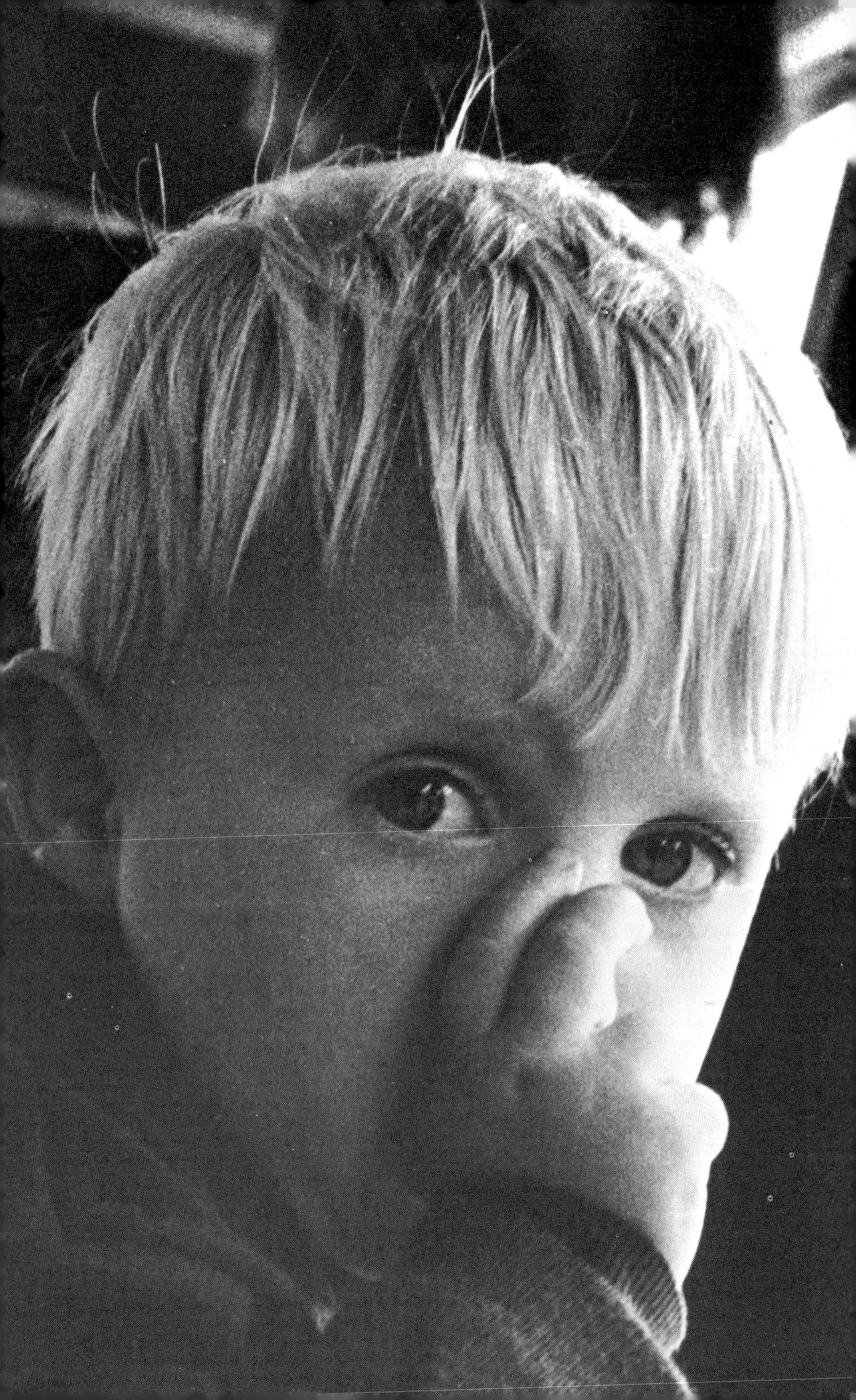

"How did you hurt your finger, Mommy?" the boy asked.

"I was working out some angry feelings I had about Grandma," his mother said.

"Why?" the boy wondered. "What did she do to make you mad? We haven't even *seen* her since last summer."

"It was things Grandma did a long time ago," said the mommy. "Things she did that made me mad when I was little like you are now. But when I was little I didn't show my feelings the way you do now. Getting mad, the way you do, is better, don't you think?"

"I guess it is, Mommy," said her son. "If people didn't know how to be angry they wouldn't be human, would they?"

Jane Howard

The person is a set of interpersonal
relationships,
and it is during infancy that the pattern
which these relationships shall take
is largely determined. . . .
Without the state of infant dependency
human love would not be what it is,
and without those affective bonds
which tie one human being to another
it is more than doubtful
whether there could ever have been
any future for the human species.

Ashley Montagu

Touching with love

Love means being full of life. We wonder at the depths of feeling we experience in loving contact with a very special other. In love we can really touch another person and really get in touch with our total body.

What is this need
To touch your face?
As if I were blind
I reach to touch your face;
You move, just out of reach.

If we had never been lovers,
Would you mind so much?
If we had never been lovers,
Would I need to?

Ione Hill

Then if any device could be found
how a state or an army
could be made up
only of lovers and beloved,
they could not possibly find
a better way of living,
since they would abstain
from all ugly things,
and be ambitious
in beautiful things
toward each other;
and in battle side by side,
such troops although few
would conquer
pretty well all the world.

Plato

How am I to withhold my soul
That it not impinge on yours? How am I
To bear it beyond you toward any other?
Ah, gladly would I set it apart
As in darkness lost in some strange
Still place where it would not vibrate
Whenever in your depths it vibrates,
But everything we are touched by, you and I,
Draws us together as the stroke of a bow
Mingles two strings in a single note.
Upon what instrument have we been strung?
And in the hands of what musician are we held?
Oh, sweet song.

Rainer Maria Rilke

To My Wife
(Nursing Our First Born)

As
you sit
with child at breast
settled against a pillow
letting his soft mouth
milk the mother of you
draining
the full breasts
flat,
I dream your wild
flesh fresh
burning me in you
the night
the virgin
burned to life
the man.
You then
and
you now
and both
I love.

Richard M. Prodey

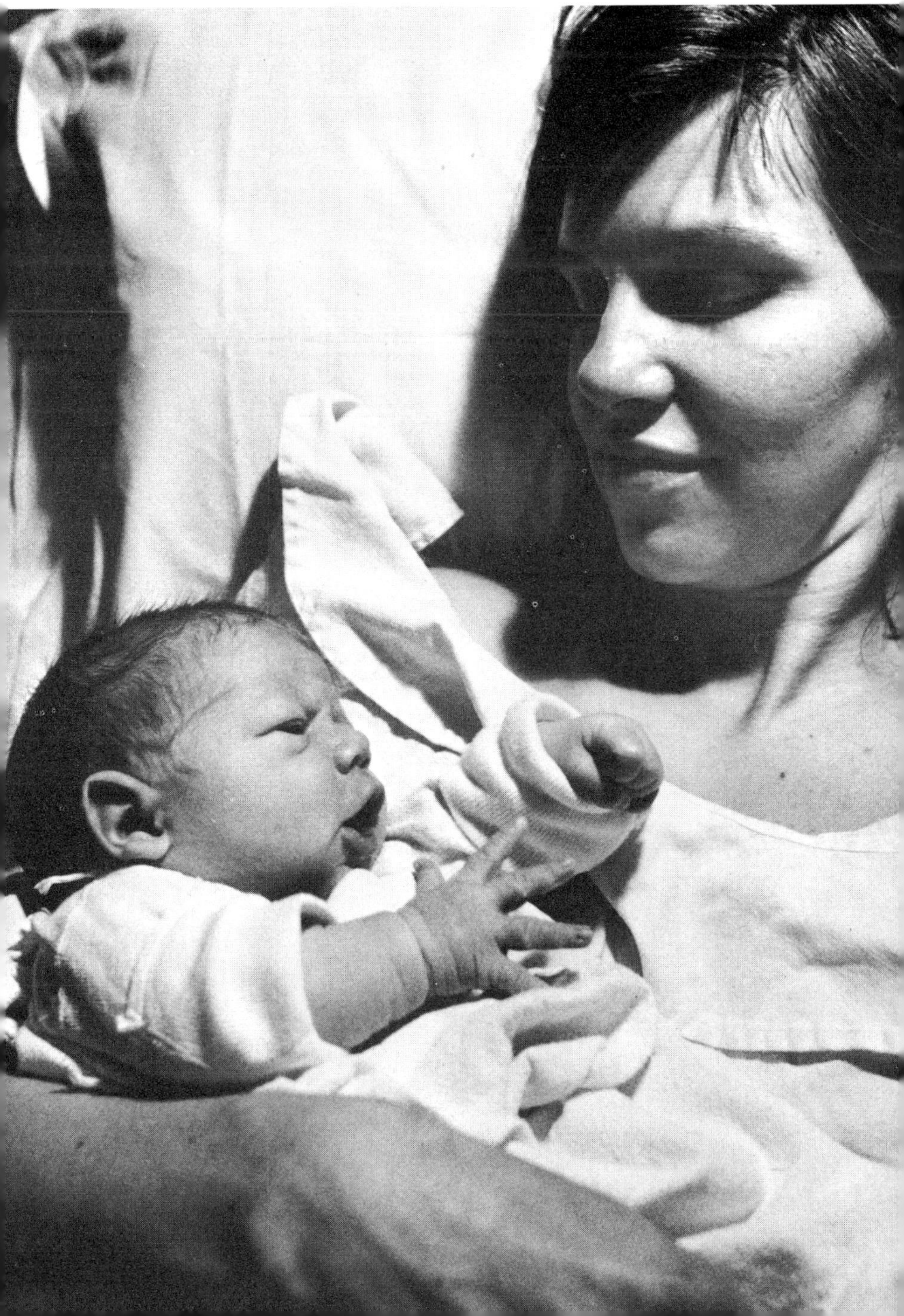

The most submissive thing in the world can ride roughshod over the hardest in the world—that which is without substance entering that which has no crevices.

Lao Tzu

Silence is the element
in which great things
fashion themselves together,
that at length they may emerge,
full-formed and majestic,
into the daylight of life,
which they are henceforth to rule.

Maurice Maeterlinck

Doing things with love

Ultimately touch aims at becoming whole, having everything all together, doing everything we do in a loving spirit. We are reintegrated, reorganized, at one with our complete self and all our activity.

Things are produced around us,
but no one knows the whence.
They issue forth,
but no one sees the portal.
Men one and all
value that part of knowledge
which is known.
They do not know
how to avail themselves
of the unknown
in order to reach knowledge.

Chuang-tzu

Sometimes it seems to me that it doesn't matter what I do, that it is enough to exist, to sit somewhere, in a garden for example, watching whatever is to be seen there, the small events. At other times, I'm aware that other people, possibly a great number of other people, could be affected by what I do or fail to do, that I have a responsibility, as we all have, to make the best possible use of whatever talents I've been given, for the common good. It is not enough to sit in that garden, however restful or pleasurable it might be. The world is full of unsolved problems, situations that demand careful, reasoned, and intelligent action.

Robert Kennedy

PETE'S TAVERN

If you have not made life
a little richer
and its conditions
a little more just
by your living
you have not touched the world.

David Starr Jordan

People often want above all else
to be safe,
so they get hooked into situations
where only predictable things happen,
where they can play
structured games with each other.
Most marriages aren't bad,
they're just kind of gray,
because people have shut off
so much of themselves
from each other.
We're bored
because parts of our spectrums
aren't exposed.
If you can expose
something in your spectrum
that's been concealed,
it can't help but enrich the system.
Our artfulness
is to get this to happen
in small enough doses
so that people can manage the exposure.

James V. Clark

You don't have to be sick to get better.

Jane Howard

Spontaneous love

Things like joy and love are not experiences that can be programmed or commanded at will. They must be allowed. We must let it happen, discover what love really means, bridging the gulf of flesh and blood and bones between humans.

Temporary relationships
should be less fraught
with guilt and other pain
than they are.
Our whole society
is set up to make you think
"marry him
or it's a waste of time,"
but temporary relationships
are what suit some people.
The key,
no matter how long it lasts,
is to enjoy it,
be honest,
and not deceive
each other.

William Schutz

Not only
Skin-naked
Juxtaposition,
But any other
Naked relationship,
Depends upon
The taking off;
Completely naked
Is without fear.

Come, let us
Take off
Each other's
Armor.

Ione Hill

Sexuality is an attitude
toward life,
a state of being.
To be alive sexually
is to regulate
your own sexuality
for deepest pleasure.

Stanley Keleman

Love properly understood, . . .
occurs only between virgins.
What does virginity mean?
I will tell you.
Pure, unsullied, . . .
not yet used for any purpose.
Note the word *use*.
It cannot exist in love
or in the sexual act.
Use implies a destruction of value.
It implies that this is a contact
that depreciates the flesh.
This, I will tell you, is not so!
Love exists without man or woman.
Participation in this never-born,
never-ceasing love
is possible for man and woman
through the wondrous commingling
of their minds and bodies.
In this world of Maya, or illusion,
we must recognize the truth;
for those who are pure
the sexual act is a perpetual renewal
of virginity.

Robert H. Rimmer

But if you love
and must needs have desires,
let these be your desires:
To melt and be like a running brook
that sings its melody to the night.
To know the pain
of too much tenderness.
To be wounded
by your own understanding of love;
And to bleed willingly and joyfully.

Kahlil Gibran

Do you not know that your body
is a temple of the Holy Spirit within you,
which you have from God?
So glorify God in your body.

1 Corinthians 6:19-20

Being in love

Love is meant to be as normal to us as breathing, an integral part of life. Being in love is a most powerful experience for human growth. Lovers are not afraid to live, not afraid to share the glory of the human condition.

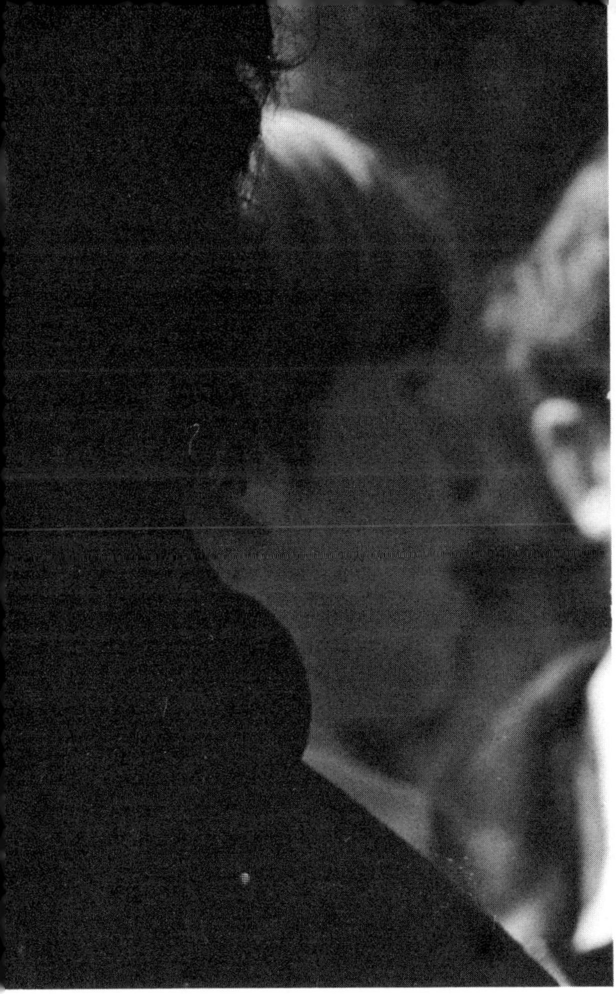

You and I,
are we not the same? . . .
Sometimes I cannot tell
myself from other people. . . .
It seemed to me as though
I no longer existed
in my own person alone,
as though I were one
with the all.

R. D. Laing

My generation is tired of defining man
in terms of his differences;
it wishes to look at another
in terms of common factors:
that which we can share,
that which will bring us together,
rather than that which isolates.
The mind divides, the body unites;
we're learning to touch again
in order to escape the hypnotism
of overcerebralization.
The danger in overemphasizing this
can be seen in crowds:
touch without responsibility,
and the ability of a psychopath
such as Hitler
to utilize their energy.

Ira Einhorn

I have perceiv'd that to be with those I like
 is enough,
To stop in company with the rest at evening
 is enough,
To be surrounded by beautiful, curious, breathing,
 laughing flesh is enough,
To pass among them or touch any one, or rest
 my arm ever so lightly round his or her
 neck for a moment, what is this, then?
I do not ask any more delight, I swim in it as
 in a sea.
There is something in staying close to men and
 women and looking on them, and in the
 contact and odor of them that pleases
 the soul well,
All things please the soul, but these please
 the soul well.

Walt Whitman

He who sees all beings in the Self,
and the Self in all beings, hates none.

Ilsha Upanishad

Because there is one bread,
we who are many are one body,
for we all partake of the one bread.

1 Corinthians 10:17

As kingfishers catch fire, dragonflies draw flame;
As tumbled over rim in roundy wells
Stones ring; like each tucked string tells, each
    hung bell's
Bow swung finds tongue to fling out broad
    its name;
Each mortal thing does one thing and the same;
Deals out that being indoors each one dwells;
Selves—goes itself; *myself* it speaks and spells,
Crying *What I do is me: for that I came.*

I say more: the just man justices;
Keeps grace: that keeps all his goings graces;
Acts in God's eye what in God's eye he is—
Christ—for Christ plays in ten thousand places,
Lovely in limbs, and lovely in eyes not his
To the Father through the features of men's faces.

Gerard Manley Hopkins

PERINCIOLI
•RÖRSWIL